D1613400

Pebble® Plus

Snakes

Copperheads

by Mary R. Dunn

Consultants:
Christopher E. Smith, M.Sc., A.W.B.
President, Minnesota Herpetological Society
Gail Saunders-Smith, PhD,
consulting editor

CAPSTONE PRESS
a capstone imprint

Pebble Plus is published by Capstone Press,
1710 Roe Crest Drive, North Mankato, Minnesota 56003.
www.capstonepub.com

Library of Congress Cataloging-in-Publication Data
Dunn, Mary R.
Copperheads / by Mary Dunn.
p. cm.—(Pebble plus. Snakes)
Summary: "Simple text and full-color photographs describe copperhead snakes"—Provided by publisher.
Audience: 005-008.
Audience: K to grade 3.
Includes bibliographical references and index.
ISBN 978-1-4765-2071-1 (library binding)
ISBN 978-1-4765-3484-8 (eBook PDF)
1. Copperhead—Juvenile literature. I. Title.
QL666.O69D86 2014
597.96'3—dc23   2013007428

Editorial Credits
Jeni Wittrock, editor; Kyle Grenz, designer; Eric Manske, production specialist

Photo Credits
Alamy: Norman Owen Tomalin, 15, Phil Degginger, 21, Shaun Cunningham, 7; Corbis: cultura/Callista Images, 11; Dreamstime: Fotandy, 1; Getty Images: Photo Researchers/E R Degginger, 17, Visuals Unlimited/Jim Merli, 19; James P. Rowan, 9; Newscom: DanitaDelimont.com/Joe & Mary Ann McDonald, 13; Science Source: Nature's Images, 5; Shutterstock: Jason Patrick Ross, cover, vlastas66, design element (throughout)

Note to Parents and Teachers

The Snakes set supports national science standards related to biology and life science. This book describes and illustrates copperhead snakes. The images support early readers in understanding the text. The repetition of words and phrases helps early readers learn new words. This book also introduces early readers to subject-specific vocabulary words, which are defined in the Glossary section. Early readers may need assistance to read some words and to use the Table of Contents, Glossary, Read More, Internet Sites, and Index sections of the book.

Printed in the United States of America in North Mankato, Minnesota.
032013   007223CGF13.

Table of Contents

Slithery Snakes

A copperhead snake

lies curled in a woodpile.

A hidden copperhead feels safe.

But if you bother it, watch out!

Copperheads are quick to bite.

Copperheads live in
North America. They make
dens in woodpiles, holes in
the ground, and other small,
dark places.

Copperhead Range

☐ where copperheads live

North America

Europe

Asia

Africa

South America

Australia

Antarctica

N
W — E
S

Up Close!

Copperheads have scaly bodies with dark and light markings. Copperheads are 1.7 to 3 feet (0.5 to 0.9 meter) long.

Copperheads have two

large fangs and big jaws.

They smell and touch

with their forked tongues.

Finding Food

Copperheads hunt at night. Their heads have special pits to find food. Pits sense the heat of mice, small birds, and other prey.

Copperheads bite prey with their fangs. Venom in the fangs makes animals quiet and easy to eat. Copperheads swallow their prey whole.

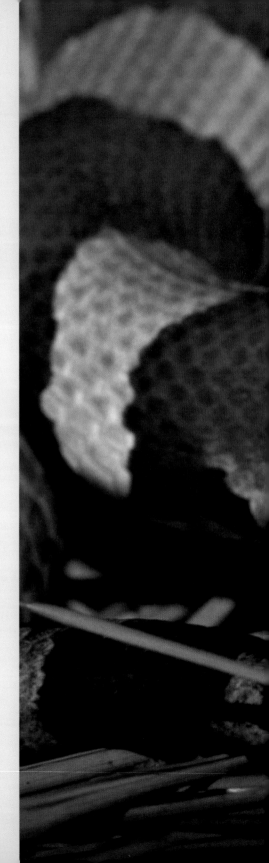

Growing Up

Female copperheads have broods of 2 to 10 babies. Babies are born in a thin sac. Each baby weighs less than 1 ounce (28 grams).

Young copperheads have yellow-tipped tails. Frogs and toads see the yellow tail. When they hop closer, the young snake catches its meal.

Staying Safe

People are copperheads'
worst enemies. They kill
copperheads or ruin their dens.
If copperheads stay safe,
they can live up to 18 years.

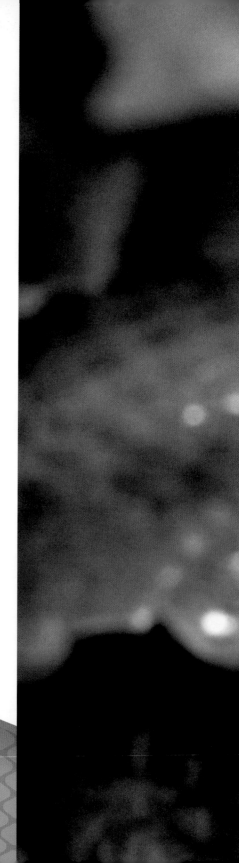

Glossary

brood—a group of animals born at the same time to the same mother

den—a small, hidden place where a wild animal lives

fang—a clawlike tooth; copperheads' fangs squirt out venom

forked—split from one part into two parts

prey—an animal that is hunted by another animal for food

scaly—covered in many small, hard pieces of skin called scales

venom—a liquid poison made by an animal to kill its prey

Read More

Braidich, Victoria. *Copperhead.* Killer Snakes. New York: Gareth Stevens Pub., 2011.

Gunderson, Megan. *Copperheads.* Snakes. Edina, Minn.: ABDO Pub., 2011.

Sexton, Colleen. *Copperheads.* Snakes Alive. Minneapolis: Bellwether Media, 2010.

Internet Sites

FactHound offers a safe, fun way to find Internet sites related to this book. All of the sites on FactHound have been researched by our staff.

Here's all you do:

Visit *www.facthound.com*

Type in this code: 9781476520711

Super-cool stuff!

Check out projects, games and lots more at
www.capstonekids.com

Index

Word Count: 195
Grade: 1
Early-Intervention Level: 17